Advanced Kuji-in

Transformational Approach

by MahaVajra

F.Lepine Publishing

http://www.kujiin.com

ISBN: 978-1-926659-26-8

Table of contents

History and Variations

The Nine Hand Seals Technique and its related teachings have their origins in the Hindu religion where they were initially used by a few groups from the lower castes. These mystical techniques were a means used by the monks to bring the virtues of the spirit into mundane experience. The original form was not as developed as the system we have today. Thus, this historical perspective refers to the origins of the current system, not the modern Nine Hand Seals Technique as it exists today. Buddhism came out of Hinduism, and, with it, the Nine Hand Seals Technique became ever more popular. The original mudras remain the same as those taught in ancient times, but Buddhist mantras were also added to the system to enhance it. The original mantras were in Sanskrit. They are invocations and celebrations of the various Buddhas. The Buddhist movement later traveled to China, where the tradition was passed on to the hermetic and esoteric groups extant there. Boa Pu Zhi, a wise Chinese master, was the first to put the nine hand mudras on paper, in his work published around the 3rd century AC. Eventually, the techniques migrated to Japan, along with esoteric Buddhism, where the mantras were translated into Japanese phonetics.

The modern Kuji-In technique is composed of a ritual process comprising the traditional application of the Buddhist "three secrets" (mudra, mantra, and mandala). The true Kuji-In secret lies within the contemplation of that philosophy which we use to change our attitude about life. The goal of Kuji-In practice is not to acquire strength, control, healing powers, telepathy, etc... These are only side effects of practicing the rituals and focusing a bit on the governing philosophy. Most people learn the technique simply to attain one or more of these powerful side effects. By aiming at such a mundane goal, their limited focus will ultimately result in the attainment of 1/10th of what they could have achieved by practicing Kuji-In to the fullest. The real path of Kuji-In is the quest to know the truth about ourselves. It is a contemplation of higher principles, an application of noble behavior to our daily lives, and it requires the mental ability to perceive knowledge that is not studied, but revealed. Once a revelation occurs, the side effects mentioned earlier will develop rapidly and without effort.

A Kuji-In teacher transmits these techniques according to his own experience of its revelations. Since the technique was transmitted orally to many different groups, by many different masters, the organization of the root knowledge remains the same, but the ritual aspect has changed somewhat over time.

Thus, there is no dramatic change in the system, because the true knowledge of Kuji-In is acquired through revelation, and the various ritual techniques inevitably stimulate the mind towards the same goal, which is the revelation of truth. As long as the ritual practice is applied, the side effects eventually manifest. The general public sees the manifestation of these side effects as the most obvious sign of the attainment of mastery and generally (and mistakenly) believes that they are the intent of these practices.

Some Kuji-In practitioners are adepts of meditation, and, according to them, the Kuji-In technique is a way to deepen meditation. Other Masters are Adepts of the martial arts, and, for them, the Kuji-In techniques build the profound inner powers of the warrior. Sorcerers will say that it develops the ability to manifest magical phenomena. Peasants and farmers might say it is the technique used to attract good fortune and stimulate good crops! Those who speculate on such matters suggest that there might be around 4000 different schools practicing these techniques around the world, each transmitting the technique with their own unique variations. Some Buddhists use a Qi Gong dance along with the 9 syllables, while others sit still in meditation and use a longer version of the Nine Mantra prayers. The application of the principles doesn't matter. As long as the

Kuji-In philosophy is the proper foundation of the ritual technique, the desired results will be attained.

It is crucial to receive the teachings, techniques and philosophy of Kuji-In from a competent teacher. Although you could read the technical details of the practice in any book related to this system, only the insight and guidance of an experienced teacher will bring about an understanding of the attitude that is necessary to stimulate the requisite revelation process in the student. The revelation of such knowledge is not a conscious process and cannot be logically reasoned from the facts at hand. A competent teacher is therefore one who has personally experienced the phenomena of inner revelation repeatedly over a number of years. Although we might also say that a competent teacher has learned the techniques by himself (and that would be partially true), it would shed doubt on the competence of the teacher to suggest that he or she has ONLY learned these techniques by him or herself. In fact, the most important factor in this learning is the guidance that the practitioner receives in order to attain the state of revelation. This revealed knowledge is simply validated by the teacher, so the student does not doubt their first experiences. Later on, if the student has some competence in pedagogy, and has acquired enough of a deeper understanding of the technique over the years to merit it, he might become a teacher himself.

In order to help you to discern a good teacher from a pretender: A competent Kuji-In teacher must believe in God. He meditates often, and has done so for many years. He will emphasize the importance of the philosophy and its contemplation, (not the lower forms of accomplishment). He will have great self-confidence without being egotistical. He will generally be in a state of harmony, but will accept himself to the fullest even in times of personal turbulence. He will have a passion for life and he will inspire you. He will require an exchange for his guidance, for he knows about the laws of Karma and responsibility. A good teacher will not brag about his competence. He will tend to keep his spirituality to himself, and for his students. Most of all, we recognize a tree from its fruits. If you are having a fruitful experience from learning with a particular teacher, then that teacher is competent. When you are certain you have outgrown what a teacher can offer you, seek a higher source of knowledge.

Transformational Approach

The kuji-in technique you will learn in this book is the *transformational approach*. It is a technique that has been thought for ages in spiritual temples, from master to disciple. Although the ritual technique is almost the same as the Japanese Mikkyo tradition, the most important aspect is the personal transformation aspect that was more popular in the Indian and Chinese Buddhist version. In a sense, this technique addresses itself to a large public, since it provokes a transformation for the holistic healer as well as the martial arts adept. Nevertheless, only a few people will have the courage and discipline to apply the technique and consider the philosophical aspects.

This approach of the kuji-in technique is blunt and direct. It requires the implication of the complete being, with an attitude of acceptance and humility. Its core substance is about the transformation of the self, at the level of the body, the mind, and the spirit. We encourage you to ponder each chapter of this book thoroughly before you go on to the next. Take your time to practice and contemplate the suggested *ways of life*.

Invocative Technique

The Kuji-In techniques as they will be shown to you here should initially be practiced in the invocative manner, meaning that they will utilize an active and lively call for Spirit to become available to our human consciousness. Therefore the invocation is said aloud, while you breathe actively, and while you move; thus a certain sum of energy is put into each aspect of this practice.

With a calm demeanor, without breathing too rapidly, it is recommended that, the first time you practice Kuji-In, you manifest your joy that you are alive and happy. Vigorously vocalize the mantras, (without shouting). Allow your body to move to the rhythm you set for your practice, even during the seated portions of practice. You may also shake your hands back and forth while holding the mudra, and then move your hands back to the fixed position in front of you, at the level you find comfortable.

Before you begin a Kuji-In practice period, stretch your body, drink a bit of water, sit down, and begin the "air and energy breathing" technique. It is essential to perform this technique before every Kuji-In session to ensure it will be maximally effective.

The Air and Energy Breathing Technique

There is a lot of free energy circulating in the air and space around you. This useful energy is called Prana; it is as subtle as air, and it is constantly used by your energetic body. When you inhale, you naturally draw air and Prana into your nose. The air goes down into your lungs. The Prana takes another route. It travels along the inside of your nasal cavity and up inside the cranial vault. When the Prana reaches the top of your spinal column, it splits and travels down either side of your spine. As you inhale, the air and Prana naturally flow along the correct path, without effort or concentration on your part. Unfortunately, many of us have obstructions that prevent Prana from flowing to its natural destination. To clear out these obstructions, it is helpful to use the following visualization in concert with the exercise of air and energy (prana) breathing:

- Breathing in, visualize the Prana flowing into your nasal cavity, and then flowing up into the inside of your cranial vault as a 2-3" wide stream of white energy.

- From there it travels to the top of the inside of your cranial bone, to the back of your head, and then splitting to flow down either side of your spinal column.

- At the tailbone (coccyx) it continues on to your perineum, (the tender spot between your anus and sexual organs) where it condenses its flow and enters the base chakra.

Whether you are conscious of it or not, every time you inhale air, Prana travels along at least a part of this path, depending on the health of your entire energetic system. Practice this conscious visualization along with the breathing, with clarity, but without strain. This will help the Prana flow naturally along its designated path and will clear any blockages you may have developed in those channels. Eventually, you will naturally complete the entire Prana cycle without concentrating on it. As you inhale, your body naturally retains the Prana, even though there is no valve preventing it from being expelled. Thus, it continues to travel up inside the cranial bone and along the route we have described, to the perineum, where it is absorbed into the base chakra, with each and every breath. For more information on these channels of energy, you may want to do some extra research on the Ida and Pingala channels.

It is essential to activate adequate air/Prana circulation throughout your body to get everything working correctly. When Prana flows properly, it fuels the fire in the base chakra. The fire in the base chakra flares up like a flame, and does not die down to its original level for some time, even after you finish this exercise. Fanning the flame at the base charka markedly enhances the Kuji-In awakening process. Each time you exhale, only air (mostly carbon dioxide) is expelled; the Prana remains in the body and continues to flow naturally without any mental effort on your part.

RIN

The RIN Way of Life

You have the right to live. Every time you let yourself believe you do not have the right to live, to be, to act, you are telling the Universe that you prefer being the victim of your own life events. Stand up, be confident and declare your own right to live.

On the other hand, do not give yourself permission to act arrogantly, or to say that you are better than anyone else. If you make such comparisons, you are asserting that there are different levels of the right to live, or that some people are more entitled to life, or have more right to breathe than others. When you make those kinds of comparisons, you destroy your own right to live, to be, and to feel good about yourself.

From time to time, we all give in to the tendency to admit to ourselves that we think we are better than everyone else. Yet, this erroneous thinking reinforces the negative aspects of your ego. If you want to achieve true self confidence, you must abandon all attempts at comparing the value of human life. Thus, you may certainly express your various preferences, preferring apples over cherries, or the color pink to the color blue, but it is crucial to the development of full self consciousness that you never judge others as less worthy of life than you.

Only God can judge a human being and His judgment is always: I LOVE YOU!

Once you start trusting yourself, practice projecting this trust into life. Say to yourself, "Life takes care of me, I trust life". Eventually, this practice will lead you to have faith, the awareness that God takes care of you every moment, and that you can let go of your fears and worries; you are never alone and God supports all of your actions. If He did not, you would simply cease to be.

In fact, as a human being, you don't really have any control over exactly what happens in your life, but you do have the power of choice. By following these techniques, you will gain the tools to influence the outcome of events in your life, and eventually, you will also develop the power to manifest events more as you desire them to be. You still won't have any direct control over the outcome of events in your life; you will simply learn to trust life, and to have faith. Faith releases Divine energy into your body and fuels all other spiritual activities.

RIN Technique

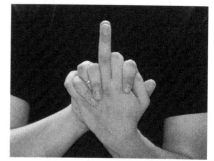

Extend your two middle fingers and interlace all other fingers.

Chakra: Base

Mantra jp: On baï shi ra man ta ya sowaka

Mantra sk: Om vajramanataya swaha

臨

Visualize a flame at your base chakra, which grows brighter each time you inhale air and Prana. The circulation of air and Prana into your body ignites and fans the flame. Strangely, the flame does not go out immediately, even after you stop this exercise; the process seems to be self sustaining. When you exhale, vocalize the Kuji-In prayer three times (3). It is at the inhalation that the flame flares up. Visualize the flame growing until your whole body seems to be filled with this spiritual fire. This is the first Key of RIN. With this sacred technique, 90 complete breaths (1 breath = 1 inhalation and 1 exhalation) set your body on fire. You can begin with 9 complete breaths, (that is 27 mantras), but to gain the full potential of the RIN Kuji, and start the path, you will have to perform the complete set 90 times every few days until you have completely mastered the technique, and you feel the energy strongly inside of you. In the first few breaths, the RIN fire simultaneously grows in the base chakra and fills your lower body and legs. As you complete the set, the RIN fire covers your entire body, legs, arms, and then extends a bit beyond your body (about one inch from the exterior surface of your skin). A bit of dark blue smoke may be seen when a part of your body is set on fire for the first few times. After that, you may see a very little bit of white smoke. Allow the smoke to drift up unnoticed; do not spend any energy attending to it.

Physical vs. Spiritual Enhancement

You must give up the belief that the physical body is not spiritual, or that the spirit is in some other place or dimension. We use the terms physical and spiritual to describe different aspects of our nature, but these different aspects both exist at the same time, and in the same place *in you*, simply on different energetic levels. Your spiritual, astral, energetic, and physical bodies are the same unique thing. They are all on the same frequency scale, differing only by their rate of vibration. Thus, anything you do on the spiritual plane flows directly down into the physical plane whether you want it to or not. Therefore, Kuji-In is a spiritual technique that yields quite powerful physical results. The RIN Kuji technique develops your ability to generate sustained energy circulation, or even intense bursts of energy when needed. This practice enhances your willpower, your mental determination, and even the electro-magnetic output of your nervous system. IF you strain with all your might to lift something, your nervous system sends out energy to your muscles to provide the necessary output strength. A normal human being's nervous system can deliver about 30% bio-electric energy to their muscles. When the RIN technique is competently performed, you can double the output of bio-electric energy to 60%, thus doubling your strength. You will still have to do some physical training to get your muscles used to handling this much of a load of energy; the delivery of 100% of your potential energy to your muscles would damage the tendons and is not a goal of this technique. Some Masters, especially in the martial arts, practice bone and tendon Qi Gong. They can lift 800 pounds in an instant and deliver powerful and deadly blows with their fists. If you can lift 200 pounds, and you do any form of muscle conditioning (body building) to increase your strength to

400 pounds, you can use the RIN technique to double it again to 800 pounds. Of course, you won't accomplish that by just using the RIN technique for a few hours here and there, you have to give it time to work on your body.

RIN has many other useful applications, some which are not obvious to the beginner. One thing is certain, if you do not develop your proficiency with the RIN technique, all the other Kuji-In techniques will lack the fuel they need; the available energy for the other techniques will simply be inadequate to make them useful. If you want to use these techniques to heal others with the SHA technique for example, the improved energy circulation that RIN, KYO and TOH provide are mandatory before SHA can be utilized effectively. RIN will give you the strength you need at every level, because your spirit does not see any difference among your physical, ethereal, astral, mental, causal, soul, and spiritual energetic selves, aside from the variable frequencies they each represent. Everything that comprises you is one single entity with a dense physical body at the lowest frequency.

A Quick Burst of Energy

If you ever need a quick burst of physical energy, you may apply this simple technique, once you have the RIN fire coursing through you. This technique will be totally useless to anyone who does not practice the Kuji-In system you are learning.

Get the RIN fire coursing through you in 3 breaths, then focus joyful energy into your base chakra, spreading it throughout your entire body. Joy is the foundation of life, and releasing this emotion will trigger a vigorous energy flow. Next, tense every muscle in your body and hold that tension for 3 seconds. Tensing your muscles will condense the energy, pooling it for your use. Then, release the tension without relaxing your muscles completely and hold that for 3 seconds, and then tense and hold for 3 seconds again. Joy is life, and the increase in life energy in your system will cause your internal energy to circulate more vigorously. This pumping (tense-release) action floods your body with bio-available physical energy. Repeat this sequence several times. With each repetition imagine that you are pulling higher and higher levels of vibrations into your body. It is almost as if the energy squirts into your system, as might squeeze juice from a lemon or orange into a glass. You fill yourself up with this delicious energy and it is nourishing and filling. Stretch your body; open your eyes wide; look up for 3 seconds and take a deeeeep breath. Look down and take another deeeeep breath.

Resumed:

Three (3) complete inhalations reactivates the RIN Fire in your body. Three (3) seconds of the pumping action (tensing and releasing your muscles) condenses your bio-available energy. Stretch your body again; keep your eyes opened, breathe while you look up and then down. Do not relax, after all, you asked for more energy!

KYO

KYO Way of Life

To activate the abilities of the KYO level technique, you should contemplate the following facts:

- You receive from life what you put into it.
- Every action you perform has a consequence.
- Everything you do sends out energy that will eventually return
- There is no good or evil, only action-reaction.
- You are responsible for everything that happens to you.
- You are the Master of your life.

A person must actively perform good and responsible actions for a long time before the (seemingly) bad luck stops manifesting. There are also consequences that come to you as 'awkward events', which are a result of the actions of your subconscious mind. You may believe that you have been good and responsible in your actions; however, bad luck, and disturbing events are not always a punishment for misbehavior or irresponsible action which comes about as a consequence of karmic law. Sometimes these disturbing events are the simply the result of the actions of your subconscious mind, which can be triggered into bringing these difficult events into your life when you dwell on the belief that you don't deserve to live, the belief that you are a bad person, the belief that you do not have value., etc... Rather that perpetuate this thinking and its destructive effects on the subconscious, it is possible to use these experiences as a life transforming tool. You begin this process when you accept that you are responsible for everything that happens in your life, whether you know it or not.

It may be hard to believe but you are the absolute Master of your life. Yet, how can you become powerful if you are continuously sustaining the belief that things in your life are constantly out of your control; that you have no effect on your life circumstances? To come to grips with your true nature, you must begin to struggle with the appearances that create this illusion. That illusion is your physical mask. You must grapple with it. Thus, it would be correct to say that there are events that occur for reasons you don't understand, and there are certainly energies and events set in motion around you that you are not consciously aware of, but then you are not yet fully conscious, and you must grasp that you are actually the Master of everything that happens to you, whether you KNOW it, or not. You may feel powerless about all of this at the beginning, and that is natural. It is essential to reprogram your thinking so you take responsibility for everything that happens to you. If you do not believe this; if you do not practice this, you will not gain the power to manifest what you truly want. As long as you hold on to the victim-stance programming you are currently using, you will be blaming others or life or circumstances for what manifests in your life. As soon as you realize that your change of mental attitude will ultimately have a positive effect, the temporary setbacks and hindrances can be dealt with, without giving in to self defeat and victim stance.

KYO Technique

Extend your index fingers and bend your middle fingers over your index fingers so that the tip of your thumbs are touching. Interlace all your other fingers.

Chakra: Hara/Navel

Mantra jp: On isha na ya in ta ra ya sowaka

Mantra sk: Om ishaanaya yantraya swaha

兵

The first part requires an exchange of energy between the inner and outer energetic bodies at the level of the navel chakra (2 inches below your navel, inside your body). Visualize white light flowing outward in every direction from the navel chakra, at the same time that white light energy is flowing into your navel center. The system we are describing here involves a complete circuit: input, circulation of energy – and output. This can be visualized as a single sphere with bi-directional flow, which extends out from your body just a few feet. Your inner navel is the center of the sphere (where energy comes in). You may visualize the light flowing more intensely at the front and back of your body, where the navel chakra has its entrance. (You might think of this as an input port, if that helps). Maintain the visualization and sensation of the RIN fire burning throughout your entire system as a background, but don't concentrate on it. Focus your attention on the continuous inflow and outflow of energy from your navel chakra, which then condenses into a sphere around you, and a glowing energy center inside of you. Visualize this white light flowing in and out of you, purifying your exchanges of energy with the Universe. Breathe deeply and relax. When you inhale, focus on the flow of energy into you. When you exhale, chant the full mantra prayer three times.

Conscious Evolution with Kuji-in

When you are consistently performing the philosophical contemplation described above, you will begin to see changes in your personal life. Everyone has tiny balls of clogged energy that obstruct one or more of their energetic channels. Your use of the Kuji-In techniques will enhance your spiritual experience by safely and effectively clearing out those obstructions, one or more at a time. The material that was clogging your channel is then released, sent back to the Universe. Eventually, some of this dispersed energy may re-manifest the events that lead to whatever caused the blockage in the first place, offering you an opportunity to resolve this issue once and for all. Thus, even though the energy 'clogs' are dispersed into the Universe, they can result in the reappearance of previous trials and life-challenges if you have not mastered the karmic lesson associated with them.

Kuji-In is a process that allows you to release the detritus of human experience. The side effect of this release is that you become more powerful, but the primary goal is always to evolve. Once you rid yourself of energetic obstructions, you may still experience a few of these karmic occurrences, but they will inevitably be an event that you can resolve promptly, or an event your Super Conscious chose for you, in order to experiment and have new experiences in your life. In every case, you will become stronger. However, Kuji-In is not a technique that will give a human being Supernatural powers for the sake of their ego, or because of a human lust for power. Kuji-In is not intended to provide an ego-boost, and, in many instances can be quite hard on those with fragile egos: those who dwell in vanity, with the arrogance of false superiority. Rather, Kuji-In triggers an expansion of consciousness, which naturally leads to the evolution we have been describing. As you evolve, you will soon discover that the distressing events that you were hoping to resolve actually occur more frequently, sometimes following one another in rapid succession. These challenging events manifest more quickly, so you can evolve more quickly. If you currently feel overwhelmed by bad luck or bad karma, slow down; take the time you need to resolve each situation that emerges, one at a time. Kuji-In is meant to make this process easier, you will get overwhelmed only if you take on too much. Develop faith, and learn to trust in life with RIN. Develop personal responsibility with KYO. This will make your life easier.

If you find that there are a lot of negative events occurring in your life, take a bit of time to do the KYO Kuji. Contemplate the concept that you are responsible for (you are the inner cause of) everything that happens, while making the energy flow in/out at the level of the navel chakra. Even if you don't know the inner cause at the moment, by allowing yourself to be open to the concept that these painful or frustrating events come from you, the problem will be easier to resolve. If the event has been hovering on the verge of manifestation, it is also more likely to become an actual fact. Once it is actually manifested, you will notice that you have the tools to easily resolve it.

A Word About Responsibility

RIN utilizes a process of enhancing self-trust and faith. It should never be invoked to evade personal responsibility for anything. If you become aware of a problem and you choose to ignore it under the pretext that, "Life will take care of itself", well... Life will take care of you alright. You may lose everything and become a beggar,... but Life will have taken care of you, according to your own dictates. If you demonstrate a lack of respect for your own personal self worth through your failure to act, then you will manifest inaction and lack of value. As the KYO process teaches us, if you exhibit personal value and responsible action, then you will be responsible for causing what you desire to manifest (positively). You must act in accordance with your desires.

Yet, even if you work very hard at putting these principles into action, if you do not believe that Life will take care of you, responsible action may manifest as constant challenges to your security. Even when you begin to exhibit responsible action and trust in Life, it will take quite a while to manifest what you want if you do not have the RIN attitude of faith set firmly in place. These techniques build upon each other, and mastery of one technique helps you do well at the next. Thus, mastery means having each technique solidly established as part of your life, so that responsible action will help you manifest abundance in all aspects of your life (if you have faith that Life will take care of you).

Some people call this process transmuting karma; others refer to it as transcending the human experience. I call it transmuting emotion, for it is at the emotional level where the transcendence occurs. You can use your conscious mind to penetrate and absorb the emotional content and meaning of your experiences, to absorb and digest them, so they become the nutrients that help you to evolve.

An emotion cannot be transmuted by actively wishing it to go away, or trying to get rid of it. Whatever experience you are dealing with occurred so you might become aware of your deepest emotions, to face them and absorb them. It is only by becoming consciously aware of the full range of our emotional experiences that we will be able to transmute these experiences and use them to help us evolve. Our Super-consciousness intentionally experiments with (allows us to experience) these different life situations and difficult emotions, so our souls can taste life in all its wonder and misery. Our Super-consciousness is exposing us to these experiences so the conscious mind can "wake up" and become aware of its own existence. Therefore, it is not our task to flee such experiences, nor, contrarily, to seek them out. Life will bring what we need to us. The transmutation process cannot occur if we are self-absorbed in dread, fear and worry. Those emotions only lead to avoidance. This transmutation requires the that we take the first steps in learning that life will provide what we need, and we have what we need to penetrate, absorb and digest these events so that they result in our evolution.

TOH

TOH Way of Life

TOH is the Kuji attributed to harmony, but why is that?

At this level, you are encouraged to center yourself in your inner dan tian (inside your belly), and to adopt an attitude of humility, tolerance and adaptation.

When an outside force impinges upon you, you can either resist, creating a conflict and a possible impasse, or you can bow to it, adapting your outer shape to the incoming force, yielding to it. When you accept the flow of power without rigid resistance; when you humbly adapt to its flow, you will remain in a state of harmony.

Consider a little stream of water that is trying to run its course between two mountains. Even if a giant boulder fell into the stream, obstructing its flow, the stream would not complain to the rock "Move out of the way!" and attempt to force the boulder out of its way. If the power of the rock to remain is greater than the force of the water to move it, the water will humbly flow under the rock and around its sides until it passes again on its way. Even though the rock tries to damn up the water, the water does not fight the rock. It remains in a state of harmony and keeps flowing on its own way, with humility.

Learn to tolerate what is going on around you, and if it seems to affect you, humbly adapt your attitude to the new parameters. There are other times when the force of the water is much greater than any rock, but TOH is not that time and place. TOH is a state of harmony which you maintain with tolerance, humility and a spirit of forceless adaptation.

If you drop a small rock into a pond of water, the ripples will come and go. Eventually, because of the flexible and adaptive state of water, the pond will return to a peaceful mirror-like state, contemplating itself, contained in its earthly bed. Thus, the lesson of water is to peacefully contain yourself while you adapt to your environment. If you learn this lesson properly you will always be in a state of harmony and you will always have ample energy reserves.

Let's add an important detail here. If a train is coming towards you, please don't just stand there while happily believing you are peacefully 'accepting everything that happens' and that your body will adapt to the new parameters of the incoming shock. The wise choice is to adapt your physical position and get out of the way before it is too late. If there is a lot of arguing going on around you or someone is contentious with you, adapt your tolerance, negotiate as best you can, find a solution, and take whatever actions you must to resolve the situation. Adaptation does not require that you endure persistent stupidity; adaptation means moving when you need to, changing your diet when it is time, exercising to keep your body healthy, and so on. Adaptation doesn't mean adopting a slavish attitude toward someone else's point of view, or allowing yourself to get run over by a train. It means adapting your understanding and point of view to the situation, and using the least amount of energy to flow in harmony with the forces around you, while holding firm to your inner truth. If something threatens your life, preserve your life and health in any way you can.

TOH Technique

 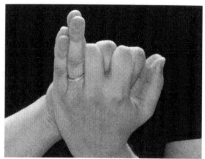

Point your thumbs and the last two fingers of both hands while keeping your index and middle fingers interlaced inside your hands.

Chakra: **Dan-tian**, between the Hara and Solar Plexus

Mantra jp: On je te ra shi ita ra ji ba ra ta no-o sowaka

Mantra sk: Om jitraashi yatra jivaratna swaha

闘

In your abdomen, among the intestines, there is a fluid substance at the physical level and a plasma fluid at the energetic level. This fluid acts like our standard battery acid, and is able to gather and store energy reserves. Your entire intestine/bowel region is filled with this energy gathering plasma. When you inhale, the oxygen rich air blows gently on the fire at your base chakra, causing this fire to flow thru your entire body; at the same time, your abdomen also fills with energy. Energy is actually flooding you from everywhere all the time, and this part of your body is constantly gathering and storing that energy, just like a battery. Whether you breathe in or out, the flow is continuous. There are no limits to the energy you can gather; an overflow is welcome. Your body will know what to do with this energy reserve, so don't be afraid to fill it. Never apply force, simply use your mind to visualize it entering and collecting, and it will fill up all by itself. Your body doesn't need much encouragement to do this, since that is its natural purpose. The energy is white when it enters and it takes on a little golden shade as it condenses within your body, filling your reserve system with healthy golden, glowing energy. Do not put any effort into immobilizing the energy. Your body naturally knows how to use it, and it might tap into the first reserves the moment you fill yourself, (if you are not used to taking the time to refill your reservoir).

After a few minutes, focus your concentration on filling up the energy reservoir in your abdomen. At the same time, let the outside world go, and begin to lose yourself in your body, as if you were wrapping yourself in a cocoon. Simply place your consciousness into your abdomen; don't worry about taking on some particular shape. Enjoy containing your consciousness in your body and isolating yourself from the outside world. Your gravity center is in your abdomen. Your life center is in your abdomen. Fill yourself with life, contain yourself as life.

This is the most important part of the TOH technique. Know that you are life. You are inside yourself, and you are not a simple human thing or mundane object, you are Life. Fill yourself with these flows of energy and be aware you are this life-giving-energy. If there is a flame going thru you (let's say it comes from the base chakra) then it fills you with life when it passes thru your body, and you become this life as consciousness. If energy flows around and throughout your entire being, then it fills you and you are that energy. If you are life, then your consciousness of yourself, which fills you all by itself, will continuously enhance your awareness of yourself as life. Be at peace, you are Life contained within yourself.

Emotional Transmutation

The emotional transmutation technique should not be done excessively. It can be demanding at first, so just begin by doing it once or twice to get the feel of it. Someday when you feel like exploring your emotional world, you may return to this exercise and practice emotional transmutation more often. You may even wait many years before you perform it regularly, it doesn't really matter. Someday, you will feel the need to use this technique. When you do, you will double your Kuji-In efficiency. Until then, a lot of things can enhance your Kuji-In efficiency, so it's ok to prefer one technique over another. It is important to try each technique at least once, and then you should focus on the main Kuji-In thread (the attitude/practice combination).

Now that you understand self-trust and how to abide in faith (RIN); now that you are responsible for what happens and you can activate the release of evolutionary experiences (KYO); now that you know you are within yourself as consciousness (TOH), you might want to know how to process all these new experiences.

When a disturbing experience occurs and you want to resolve it, first take all the necessary physical actions that you must, in order to correct the situation, then you can always work at the emotional level to go thru the entire experience (using consciousness to penetrate the experience and absorb it); by this means you can digest the experience and transform it, thus releasing the need for the experience to manifest physically again and again. This is what some teachers call "the transmutation of karma" or "transcending the human experience". I call this the Transmutation of Emotion.

An emotion is not transmuted by actively wishing it to go away, or trying to get rid of it. Every experience occurs so that you may become aware of it; it is only by consciously becoming aware of the full experience that the emotion will be transmuted and released as a new (higher) experience. We experiment with emotions so that the soul can taste life and so that consciousness can know its own existence. We must not flee from painful or difficult emotions, yet we must not intentionally provoke pain either. This process cannot take place while you listen to the inner voice and its natural fear of feeling pain. You will have to be courageous and go beyond your fear; have faith, release control over the emotional pain and become aware of the emotion without engaging it in any way.

The Transmutation Technique

Begin the Transmutation Technique by selecting some recent event that you feel guilty about or perhaps some event that left you feeling rejected. You may choose any memory, whether in your recent or remote past, as long as it is not an experience you associate with overwhelming painful emotions of any kind. Begin with this problematic, but bearable emotion, so you can do the emotional work and still be able to follow along with these three simple steps. Remember that you only need to understand and practice these steps in order to Master them.

First step (inner contact): Refresh your memory of the emotion and the situation linked to it. Take a deep breath and feel this emotion without limitation. It is in your belly, within you, and you can feel it more and more. Do not amplify it from your normal stance as the victim of this emotion, instead, listen to it, feel whatever it brings up for you, taste its flavor, accept its shape and form and how it defines itself (even if that is different than how you were defining it), contemplate it, and hold it within you. Be at peace and relive the emotion for a few breaths, up to one full minute. Be at peace. Later in your training you may perform this with some more powerful emotions. For now, just enjoy peacefully contemplating the positive change you just made.

Rarely, you may feel the need to express an emotion outwardly, in order to release some pressure that seems to be building up. On those rare occasions, (and this is not to be done frequently), simply release what you need to let go of, but never lose control over this experiment. When you are just learning these techniques, it is too easy to revert to victim stance, and to begin amplifying how terrible the situation is. Remember that you are practicing just becoming aware of the emotion. When you are unable to bear the intensity of an emotion, you may release some of the pressure on you; then just continue on with the process. It is obviously not the goal to keep this emotion trapped inside of you, or buried; rather it is the goal of this exercise to release the hold you have on it. Thus it is perfectly fine to perform the process while expressing some normal human emotion. Simply keep track of the experiment without losing your grip on the process. Breathe into your abdomen throughout the entire process. Do not breathe from your upper torso. Hold the situation that caused the emotion in your mind while you feel the emotion.

Second step (integration): Get inside the emotion and follow wherever it leads you. Breathe deeply and comfortably. As the air flows into your abdomen, your task, as consciousness, is to penetrate the emotion and let it absorb you. Be aware of all the feelings that entering this emotion evokes for you, whether you feel pain or emptiness, coldness or heat, anger or sadness- get inside of it and become it. The process of Integration requires a conscious fusion of you and the emotion. You are going to allow yourself to be enveloped within the emotion; to be integrated by it. For a few minutes, breathe and accept, breathe and become, breath and feel. Follow the path this emotion leads you on, and you will notice that most of the time, the emotion will be covering another emotion that is buried beneath it.

Every emotion arises into our consciousness because it is linked with some human experience. Use your mind to follow these experiences from the past so that you can remember what happened. You might run thru a few events (while following your emotions), until you come to the first time in your life that you felt that emotion. Stay focused. Do not jump from one thread to another; trace one experience to its root cause, following one thread at a time. As you allow the emotions to exist, without avoiding them or rejecting them, the emotion is freed up, and the energy associated with it ceases to be trapped; the emotion is alive again, emancipated. When you stop blocking it and permit it to BE, your consciousness can understand the profound essence of that emotion.

During the exercise of becoming the emotion, this previously problematic feeling will be re-set to a peaceful, natural state and you will get an abstract but clear understanding of your human experience. You are what you experience, as consciousness, as spirit, as life. Do not rush through your experience of this step. Allow the penetrating fusion to continue for a while, until there is no pain associated with the emotion, -only the experience of it. Conscious breathing will also naturally relax your hold on the emotion until it is released. Please understand that the emotion will not leave you, it will simply be free to remain inside of you without any of the previous negative associations. Always consciously push past your fear of pain; never push away the emotion. With your mind, consolidate the entire experience, which is comprised of all of the life events that made it; breathe and be conscious within that entirety.

The human ego has strong natural defense systems. Many times, the emotion is not blocked all by itself. Instead, the human ego keeps control over it, out of arrogance, vanity, jealousy, and envy, the ego refuses to allow the emotion the right to be resolved, all because of pride. You have to be in charge of this experiment and release the mental hold you keep on your emotion. You simply have to let go.

Third step (liberation): When you feel completely saturated with the emotion you are working on, when your consciousness has transmuted it into a living experience, that emotion (and all the energy that was trapped with it) is freed up. It is not released outside of you, it is available to you again, and all the power and potency of the emotion is alive for you again. The heavy, dense or contracted energy that was troubling you is released in that it is converted into its essence, and dissolved in your higher consciousness. A good feeling will naturally bubble up from within you. You may feel deeply satisfied, or you may experience a profound state of peace, or you may feel the emancipating joy of freedom. Breathe and allow this new feeling of joy fill you up, release this positive emotion if you wish to.

After this transmutation, the most important thing for you to do is to contemplate the wholeness of the experience as joyful life and happiness. Even if your physical human experience did not seem to change at all, your inner experience of it became one with God. Do not let your human ego steal this moment from you. It is crucial for you to rejoice within yourself, for your have tasted life at its fullest.

Sample Application

A few days before I began writing this book, I was struck with insecurity. I did a bit of RIN level Kuji, breathing in while focusing a bit on the fire visualization but mostly concentrating on the philosophy that "Life takes care of me, I am not alone, God is with me, and I trust life". I allowed myself to release my control over that feeling. I used Kuji-In to get in touch with the aspect I wanted to work on, and then I stopped the specific Kuji-In practice so I could concentrate on emotional transmutation.

At each in-breath, I let myself feel the emotion, completely aware of it, allowing myself to feel every sensation that came up, and to absorb the 'flavor' of these feelings. In order to get underneath the fear, I went down to the emotion of feeling abandoned. I sat within the emotion of abandonment in a state of complete acceptance for some time. I felt sad about the abandonment. It took a few minutes before I got to the depth of my sadness. My goal was to be conscious of it, without struggling against it, or trying to change it. I followed the experience deeper, and deeper, only to discover that I was afraid of not having enough money. In my early 20's I experimented with being a beggar. Each day I hoped to eat, and I came to understand that life is very hard. A few minutes later, after I had questioned myself more and more extensively as to why I had to go through the experience of being a beggar, I sought to remember some time in the more distant past when I had felt this same emotion. I remembered my brother stealing my toys and I suddenly realized *that* was when I started believing life would not give me what I want.

As I accepted that I have no control over my life, sitting in that knowledge and understanding it for quite a few breaths, the insecurity gradually dissolved and the emotion disappeared. In fact, it did not actually go away; it was transmuted into trust. Thus, I came to understand the entire experience, and the emotion became what I sought, thanks to the wonderful process of evolution.

It can take years of suffering for a normal human being to grasp the essence of a single lesson, and this process is rarely accomplished consciously. This lack of conscious understanding permits the negative events to re-emerge over and over. With conscious integration of an emotional experience, a few hours, · sometimes even a few minutes are enough to release the entire experience for you. Sometimes the experience does re-emerge again later, but only to be integrated at another level, and again, only a small amount of time is necessary to transmute it, compared to the natural evolution process. Some people resolve one karmic event every 10 years. Most cannot resolve more than a few lessons in their lifetime. Evolutionary beings can resolve these experiences 'in bulk' every once in a while, each time making their life easier and happier.

Responsibility vs. Guilt

If you feel something weighing on your mind, it is recommended that you apply physically responsible actions in order to resolve the situation physically, whenever possible. There will be a few things that are too broken to fix, like a damaged, but irreplaceable valuable. Whether an actual resolution is possible or not, apply the Conscious Transformation Technique and begin the Emotional Transmutation to allow yourself to feel the emotions related to this situation. You need to become aware of the emotions at the level of your soul in order to bring everything related to this experience up to consciousness, including dredging up any incidents where it could have originated in your past. You will use the Conscious Evolution Technique (Emotional Transmutation is the cornerstone of this process) to solve this problem at the soul level, where it originated. Using this soul level technique will make it easier for you to work out problems on the physical level, if any action is required. It will also free you from the paralyzing emotion of guilt.

The KYO technique is not designed to make you take on any responsibility for the things that happen to everyone else. It is a technique of personal-responsibility that deals with the sum total of everything that you experience. If what you are experiencing touches other people, then they also have to take the responsibility for their experience of that situation. In any case, never disregard your responsibility by saying "it's not my problem" if the experience is yours.

The KYO philosophy does not imply that "everything is my fault". The concept of fault and responsibility are two different things. Fault is maintained by an emotional attachment to guilt. Guilt is result of a self-judgment that you have been refusing to become conscious of. When we look at the concepts of fault and guilt, we see that the human ego tends to play the victim for what happened and wants to sink into the self-abusive, self-defeating shame of what it did. This creates a war against the self, which is maintained in order to prevent conscious awareness. Conscious awareness at every level is mandatory for personal evolution and transformation.

A responsible person does not suffer long from any experience, because he or she refuses to dwell in an emotional puddle, where the ego gets caught playing blinding games of denial. Responsibility is guilt free. It is an acceptance that the process of manifestation of experiences originates from a desire on the part of your Spirit to experience a particular life lesson through the events currently available in your circumstances. Responsibility requires acknowledging that everything happens because of an inner cause. This inner cause is inside you just waiting to be discovered. When you master this law, you will be able to consciously manifest what you want, but acknowledging your personal responsibility is a prerequisite to mastery. In any situation that brings up an emotion or elicits a reaction from you, the first thing to do is accept your responsibility for the experience and take a deep breath to become aware of what is going on inside you (emotion, reaction, thought). Take the time to develop this technique into a reflex. When an emotion rises, make it a reflex to automatically breath-in in order to embrace the experiences and feel the emotion. The actions you take from that point on will be more conscious and more powerful at every level.

SHA

SHA Way of Life

There is a good reason why the step before (TOH) is a contemplation of humility and tolerance. You are blessed with free-will, with the power to act and to accomplish whatever you wish. However, you must never think that you can harm others with your right to act. While you are not free from the moral responsibility that comes with your decision to act, and from the requirement that you respect others, you are absolutely free to make your own life- choices. As you become more and more powerful, you will feel this self-confidence in your guts. Do not slip into the habit of comparing yourself to others (building yourself up by putting others down), or ever looking down on anyone.

Any type of superiority complex you have will rise as you advance, it is inevitable. It is a normal part of this evolutionary path that your animal and ego reflexes will reveal themselves to you. Do not fight to repress them; neither should you act upon them. Take your superiority complex inside you and emotionally integrate it. Take the time to consider why you entered into a mental and emotional state of competition, of comparison. Feel the natural animal and biological defense system that makes us want to fight, to get into competition with everyone around us for more and larger acquisitions. Recognize that THIS is what drives this superiority complex. Absorb it.

You may also experience a reflex reaction that comes out of the fear that if you integrate these urges, you might lose this competitive edge, this drive for power. You might even say to yourself "I don't want to lose my drive for power!" Have no concern. If you absorb this superiority complex, you will still be driven to become powerful, but you will do so consciously, and it will stop being a competitive race with others, based on the ignorant and foolish assumption that there are limited resources for which you must contend. Since there are no limits to the resources available, (as you discovered in the RIN Kuji) you can continue to release competitive urges, while continuing to strive consciously to become everything that you are capable of.

Any time you force another person to do your will, you are violating their right to free-will. Never use force or power to change anything in another person's life. Use your abilities to make your own life better. You can pray for a person to heal, you can help others, you can protect yourself and those in need, but you may absolutely not use your power to confront or to challenge another human being. The power of SHA is enabled by the trust/faith of RIN, making you conscious of your right to act and to live.

SHA is confirmed by the awareness of personal responsibility you gained from KYO, since you are the one that manifested what happened to you. By improving yourself, you will manifest more desirable outcomes, outcomes that are congruent with your true will. By accepting that you manifest what happens in your life, you gain the power to consciously alter your experience and you learn to manifest consciously.

SHA is therefore assisted by the humility you gained in your practice of TOH. As you learn to adapt yourself to your environment, you gain the power to adapt your environment to your will. Tolerance helps your mind release irritation, allowing you to focus only on the good things, the positive outcomes you desire, thus encouraging the manifestation of those good things.

SHA teaches you that you have the right to have power. SHA offers you the lesson that you are always free to act. SHA naturally gives you back the means to exist fully, which physically manifests in the healing of your body.

The power of SHA should not be constrained. It must be allowed to flow freely within you. You can direct your willpower with SHA energy, and you may direct it to accomplish a specific purpose if you wish to, but in general, allow the SHA energy to flow harmoniously within you. As you develop the power of SHA, it will never stop flowing and it will always naturally go where you need it.

SHA Technique

Extend your thumbs, index fingers and both little fingers. Interlace your middle and fourth finger inside your hands.

Chakra: Solar Plexus

Mantra jp: On ha ya baï shi ra man ta ya sowaka

Mantra sk: Om haya vajramaantayaa swaha

者

SHA is the level where you begin to take charge of this process. It is your stepping stone to the expression of your inner power, directed will, intentional action and the manifestation of your true will. It is well known that the first phenomenon observed with the development of your SHA energy is the healing of your body. It is a fact that the active energy in your solar plexus immediately starts regenerating your body. The natural reflex of the body, when filled with active Qi, will be to reconstruct itself, to heal and to extend your lifespan.

First, help release energy blockages that may be present in the abdomen and on the border of the rib-cage. Place your hands palm down on your knees. Breath-in deeply, pulling the air into your abdomen; hold the air in for 3-5 seconds, then breath-out forcefully (AHHhhhhhh!) thru the mouth contracting all your abdominal muscles. Empty as much air as you can, and immediately release your abdomen muscles but keep your lungs empty, do not inhale yet. While your belly is relaxed and empty (no air in it) remain in this breathless state while you suck your abdomen up into your rib cage. Keep all your intestines and digestive organs pulled up into your rib cage. Hold it all in for 1 second, release the tension in your abdomen, then immediately pull your belly up into your rib-cage again for 1 second, relax the muscles, and then pull it back up again for a total of nine (9) "1 second hold and release" bursts, then breathe normally again. Perform this 3 to 9 times before moving on to the next Kuji-In technique.

As you work with the SHA Kuji-In technique (using mudra and mantra), focus on the fact that you are "in charge"; you have the active power, with all the means you need to act upon whatever choice you make; you have the right to live, the right to do what you wish, the right to experience life. As you focus on these concepts, fill your solar plexus with living power and determination in the form of raw energy, which is a circulating and radiant energy that is shining from your solar plexus. Crank up this power, feel it in your guts. See your body reconstruct and heal as you focus on your inner power. Visualize this nuclear fusion reactor which is inside of your body. See the powerful sun of the solar plexus.

Do not focus on this energy as any kind of comparative power. Never imagine being "more powerful than anyone else"… Rather, affirm to yourself, "I am powerful". You can use this affirmation, "I am power, I am life, and I always perform the right action: I have the power to act in my life, I have the life to act in power, and I am acting powerfully in my life". Always contemplate your power without stressing your body. Consider alternating periods of active theatrically powerful practice, with relaxed meditative practice. Move with your power. Speak the mantra with power and decisiveness. Contract your muscles as often you wish, and return to a state of relaxation from time to time. Power can flow thru you with harmony and peace. Complete the practice with relaxed breathing, while focusing on joy.

Healing

The healing ability which SHA enhances is the primary reason that most people want to learn about Kuji-In. Therefore, now that you are able to build up your energy properly and store it in your battery, (so you have an adequate source of energy for healing), and you have learned how to direct your energy according to your will, you are now ready to receive the application of SHA so that you can use the SHA technique to heal yourself or someone else.

Healing is always a side effect of the rectification of the various parts of your Self on the other levels of existence. Self-therapy and emotional integration will always be an important part of assisting the healing process.

As you gather all the components of this technique in your mind and prepare to start practicing SHA, you must focus your attention on beginning the process of healing. Although the SHA technique is enhanced by alternating between mild and intense applications, this must remain a background thought, because effective healing requires a singular focus on peace and harmony. Therefore, the best way to proceed is to keep your inner contemplation focused mostly on the healing of your body, while maintaining the fact that your solar plexus is radiating energy as a background thought.

Graphic pictorial language speaks to our subconscious. The following exercise uses the graphic pictorial symbolism of a fruit that has been left to rot, in contrast to a freshly picked fruit, bursting with life and juices. Visualize the cells within your body as they shift from weak, rotting, decaying cells, to plump, rich cells, filled with life, and light and always supplied with the perfect amount of nutrients and hydration. Use every sense to imagine and focus on this restoration process, (quickly leaving behind the idea of any decaying cells). Make the image of your cells beautiful and alive. You may place your focus on your entire body, or on a special organ, depending on your needs. Close your visualization with the certainty that there are only rich healthy cells remaining in your body.

Your body knows better than your mind what the correct shape of an organ for your body should be. If you seek to heal an organ, do not visualize the organ itself, as you may wind up manifesting an organ with an improper shape for your body. Simply focus on the reconstruction of the organ at the cellular level, and ask your body to heal. If you need a stronger and healthier heart, you may certainly visualize the organ conceptually as healthy and strong, using a visualization that is as close to the desired result as you can imagine. However, please refrain from adopting an attitude of control over the exact final shape; just allow your body to comply with your expressed desire and to perfectly create a healthy, strong heart for you that is perfectly shaped for your body. Use the affirmation, "My heart is healthy and strong; my heart is perfect for my body."

If you need to reconstruct a bone, for example, you might compare your visualization to a broken tree branch rectifying itself. Focus your thoughts on the bone structure reforming, instead of trying to dwell on the exact shape of the finished product. You certainly don't want to end-up with a misshapen bone. Again, you can trust that your bones have the power to rectify themselves at the cellular level. Then all you have to do is trust that your body knows exactly how to reform the bones so that they will fit your body perfectly. Therefore, you will always focus on the bone rectification process in general way, rather than the precise details. Use the affirmation, "My bone structure is perfect for my body."

It will take a lot of practice before you will be able to heal at will. However, although it does take time to develop this ability to the level of mastery, the rewards are excellent for the diligent and perseverant practitioner. After you have sufficient experience at regenerating your own body, you will be able to focus this healing process on others, in order to help them heal. In this way you can assist their natural healing process, just as you do when you work the SHA technique on yourself.

It is important that you understand that the SHA technique always works much better if the person in question actually wants to be healed. You may think this is a strange concept, but it does happen that some people want to experiment with being sick for a while. Others might seek to be ill because they feel guilty about asking to be loved unless they are ill. There are many reasons for these choices, even if they seem strange to you. Most of all you must understand that it is difficult, if not impossible, to fight against the will of someone who manifests sickness in their body so they can play the role of the victim in order to get attention. When someone gets sick, there is always an underlying reason for their choice to manifest that illness. In any case, it is wise to understand these principles if you want to help people to heal. It is also important (in fact, it is crucial for your own self preservation) that you refuse to overburden yourself with the responsibility of healing everyone. Remember that you are responsible for your own well being and self-preservation first. If you destroy your life trying to help others, you won't be there for anyone. DO not promote yourself as a healer. Take care of yourself before you try to help anyone else.

KAI

KAI Way of Life

The KAI level is associated with the Heart chakra. It is said that the ability one develops with this Kuji is intuition. In fact, intuition is a natural side-effect of the deeper understanding of the wisdom beneath intuition, which is compassion.

God created us to experience life. Your life is a manifestation of God. G-d experiences life through you. Everything that happens in your life is a blessing of the honorable consciousness that you are.

At the emotional level, the heart chakra is both an organ of perception and an emitting organ. It perceives life's experiences and transmits opinions about those experiences. Such opinions are usually called "judgments". The heart tells us what is right and what is wrong; these perceptions are part of the process that conditions our human ego.

KAI is the Kuji-In technique for perfecting your experience of Love. This Love is not only the love exchanged by mates, but the all-mighty unconditional Love of yourself and others. As you look at yourself, focus on accepting all that you are, in whatever state or condition you currently find yourself. This doesn't mean you will give up trying to improve yourself, but it would be cruel to wait until you are perfect before you accept all that you are. If you wait for perfection before you start loving yourself, you will wait forever, because loving yourself *as you are right now* is a necessary tool for the attainment of perfection.

KAI is the way of acceptance, love and compassion. By accepting yourself and all that you are, by accepting others as they are, by accepting everything that happens, you are opening the way for a greater experience of compassion. The compassion of KAI offers you a way to look at painful events, with an eye to seeing the lesson that the experience is trying to teach you. This is possible when you understand that there is a loving Spirit whose goal is your personal evolution and bliss; that Spirit is buried beneath those human masks of terror and sorrow, and hidden deep within the frustrating and challenging life experiences you have been having.

As to evil: Never seek pain, never inflict pain on others, and never work towards getting more pain. Nevertheless, you must understand that sometimes pain comes along with necessary and important evolutionary/transformative experiences. We spend entirely too much mental and emotional energy pushing painful experiences away, or wishing we had never had any painful experiences. When you experience pain, don't waste any energy denying it is there. Immediately accept the fact that you are having a painful experience and get right to work resolving the situation. Accepting the existence of pain does not mean we should permit the pain to continue hurting us. It simply indicates that we should acknowledge the fact that something hurts, and put all available resources into resolving the painful situation with virtuous actions. The sooner we get away from the human games of victimization and self-persecution, the faster we can get to the root of what is bothering us and start resolving the problem. Our human ego tends to amplify feelings of pain, hoping to attract attention and compassion from others. Please develop enough compassion for your self to release the pressure of pain at the emotional level. When a painful experience cannot be resolved or the facts of the situation cannot be changed (like when something irreplaceable breaks, or when someone we love dies), we are encouraged to accept it and see it with compassion so we can elevate our perception of life with Love. Everything happens for a reason; this is especially true when we are aware that we are responsible for our own experiences.

In any case, take the time to embrace every experience you have with Love and compassion. Get in touch with your emotions; instead of fearing pain, taste it inside you. Breathe into it. Be conscious and aware of your experience. When someone touches you gently, consciously feel it physically and emotionally. When you are touched aggressively, do the same. When you are the subject of the opinions of others, whether they tell you how good you are or how bad you are, embrace the opinion without judgment, but with compassion. There is only experience, and it is always a perfect experience.

KAI Technique

Interlace all of your fingers, with the tip of each finger pressing into the root of the facing finger.

Chakra: Heart

Mantra jp: On no-o ma ku san man da ba sa ra dan kan

Mantra sk: Om namah samanta vajranam ham

皆

The Heart chakra is the perceptive and emitting organ of the soul. As you bring your hands together in the KAI mudra, as you chant the prayer of KAI, remember that you are honoring your consciousness, your spirit, at the level of the Buddha or the Christ-consciousness. Bring yourself into a state of gratitude for everything that happens. Whether your experience is good or bad, pleasant or not, it does not matter, just focus on the good things that happen to you, no matter what.

Feel that your heart is a round luminous perceptive organ vibrating with Love. Don't give it a specific shape; let it reveal itself to you, since the shape is subtle and not as important as the state of mind you put yourself into. Focus on gratitude and happiness. See the vibration of your loving heart radiate in front of you and behind you from your back, while your heart chakra glows with Love.

All that you perceive is Love, the only comments you emit are Love. As you inhale, focus on your gratitude for everything that you have, for everything that happens to you. While you pray, you are honoring the greatness of your experience, the flavor of all things that you can taste as human and Spirit.

This technique conditions your heart and mind to think from the stance of Love so you will naturally develop compassion. It will elevate your perception of life and assist you in manifesting enjoyable experiences, while accepting whatever happens. Another side-effect is that your intuition will naturally become more obvious. You will become more sensible to life's events as you condition yourself to accept whatever happens without judgment. The only judgment that you can apply to your experiences is "I Love You", and most of the time, the YOU is yourself.

Kuji-in Meditation

With Kuji-In, we wish to attain a state of transcendence, to allow our consciousness to go to the plane of existence from which it originates and to remain there for a while. When this process is complete, our consciousness returns to us with spiritual light and "new information" specifically meant for us. In meditation we tend to lose our awareness of what actually happens when we transcend. Therefore, when we are performing Kuji-In techniques, we use a special physical and mental technique to retain our awareness of the physical plane, while simultaneously allowing our consciousness to achieve the state of transcendence. Begin to practice transcending in simple meditation, and then practice remaining aware while you transcend. This ability to remain aware is encouraged by performing a combination of physical movements and energy movements before the meditation or Kuji-In practice.

Before doing a motionless (or almost motionless) technique like Kuji-In, you may start with a series of moving Qi-Gong techniques to get your energy moving, to stretch your body, to awaken your spirit, and to activate your breathing and blood flow. This Qi-Gong exercise will help you perform the motionless techniques longer and with more efficiency. You can either perform the Dance of the Dragon, or Chinese Medical Qi-Gong right before you sit down to meditate or start your Kuji-In practice. It is important to remain awake while you meditate, and this exercise will help you so that you do not fall asleep during your practice period. When you achieve the state of transcendence, your awareness might drift in and out, but you are not sleeping. You will understand the difference with practice.

Sometimes, it is recommended that you practice Kuji-In techniques in a meditative fashion, instead of the usual active-invocative style. To use Kuji-In meditatively, sit and cross your legs, either in full lotus, half lotus, or with your right ankle over your left. Use a chair *only* if it would otherwise compromise your comfort. Keep your spine straight without putting conscious effort into the task. Allow your head to tilt forward a bit, but not to fall completely forward onto your chest. Practice all of the Kuji-In steps up to the one you are currently working on; continue to do your current exercise for a while. When you get to this Kuji-In technique (the one you are currently learning), allow the mantra to become very repetitive, then slowly shift into silent mental repetition, and hold your visualization effortlessly while breathing naturally, let your eyes close a bit, and just relax into the technique. Your hands may be lowered so that they rest on your legs; your focus may be shifted to the associated chakra, and you may allow yourself to gaze inward at your Spirit. Reduce every aspect of the technique until all parts of it (mudra, mantra, mandala, and chakra) are only whispered inside of you, to keep a little light in your mind while you let yourself go into the state of transcendence. Eventually, only the mantra will remain, slowly and softly repeated in your mind.

Remain in this very calm state for at least 15 minutes. You mind will be disturbed by small interruptions the first few times. This is an essential process that your mind has to go thru. It is a kind of cleaning up of your residual thoughts. Allow all your thoughts to wander, to go as they please, do not force them to be still, but do not encourage them either. When you notice you are drifting back into some thought process, gently return to the Kuji-In technique. Your physical body might also want to express itself through motion. The energy circuitry not used for meditation will produce unexpected itches, tickles, and perhaps even little cramps in your muscles. Attend to these physical annoyances ONLY if your comfort is really compromised. Each time you have a physical reaction to meditation, it means the energy is working on you and it is a good sign. Let the energy work to reduce the noise in your circuitry while you continue to focus on your meditation.

When you are used to doing 15 minutes of meditation daily, extend your practice time to 20, then 25, then 30 minutes. Meditation will train your mind to reduce extraneous chatter and noise, it will help you to let go. It will permit your body to become a suitable vessel for Spirit to interact with. The technique teaches your human aspect to accept your spiritual aspect so that all of your techniques will become much more efficient. While you will retain the awareness of your human existence, your consciousness will soon expand to include your spiritual existence.

JIN

JIN Way of Life

Jin has to do with developing perfect knowledge of self. Its power is accessed by our ability to listen and speak perfectly. As a side-effect of that ability to listen and speak perfectly, you might develop the psychic ability of telepathy. JIN requires listening at every level, and the ability to speak from every level. It is a life-long process to develop this ability, but you will immediately feel the enhancement in your life the moment you start paying attention to the JIN attitude in your everyday behavior. The JIN way of life takes the longest to develop of all the Kuji-In Techniques and it produces the most powerful results. It offers you an access to higher levels of consciousness, as well as an ability to transform your human experience into something greater. It comprises everything you have learned so far, experienced at the level of hearing and speech.

Perfect your ability to listen. The first obstruction to true listening is our need to compare ourselves to others, to establish ourselves as superior. Everyone has this superiority complex; it is genetic; we are born this way. Don't bother trying to argue,

"I'm not like that" because you are like that, and you will find out how true that is in the following lines: Our minds are conditioned to believe we hold the truth, and that our actual conception of truth is the best for us at the moment, which often leads us to degrade any knowledge that does not fit into our pre-establish scheme of beliefs and thought processes. Almost every time you say "I already know that", you have cut off your ability to learn anything further, by naturally blocking everything that might have been new to you, (since you are certain you already know it all).

It is recommended that you make yourself available to new information. It does not mean you will have to automatically accept whatever you hear as truth for you, but without the ability to be open to new ideas, you are certain to block out anything that could help you progress. If you deduce that some specific knowledge does not apply to you, or does not fit you at the moment, you will have plenty of time later to discard it. At the moment you are listening to someone else, remain available to the knowledge they are trying to impart.

As with the RIN mind-set, trust yourself and let down your guard. Respect all knowledge that is spoken every time it is spoken, whatever level it is spoken from, no matter who is addressing you. Pay attention to the way you listen, and grow from there. Listen to those who say stupid things to you; listen to those who tell you that you are a good person; listen to everyone and everything and trust yourself that, in the end, all will be well.

As with the KYO mind-set, be responsible for what you are. Develop your discernment, a sense of good judgment that will allow you to acquire only that knowledge which is best for you. If someone says you are stupid, before discarding that knowledge, seek inside of you to see if there is a place inside you where you are stupid. If you do your job well, you will certainly find a place such as this. By admitting that there is such a place to yourself, you will not react to this knowledge; you will be in acceptance of what you are. By getting out of the way of the information, the communication can continue in such a way that it resolves whatever provoked the comment.

Another important part of the KYO mind-set is also to admit to yourself that you are a good person when someone says that. It is important to accept both compliments and complaints. You are the one responsible for processing the knowledge and it is up to you to make the best of it.

As with the TOH mind-set, develop tolerance for what you hear, listen with care and lower your defenses. Do not rush to reply, to react, defend and to confront. When it is your turn to speak, speak. When it is your turn to listen, remain receptive and accept everything that is said. Accepting what is said is not an admission or approval of what is said to you. Acceptance allows you to acknowledge what is said, at the level it is said from, and does not imply that you must become or believe what is said to you.

As with the SHA mind-set, believe, know and understand that knowledge is power. Do not attempt to control the exchange of knowledge until it is your turn to define the exchange of knowledge. The knowledge will usually flow naturally in whatever direction it must, and when you notice the knowledge leads nowhere, or becomes too provocative, take full responsibility, and manifest a return to peaceful communication.

As you learned in the KAI mind-set, do not judge what you hear. Practice having a compassionate ear, and listening with love. If information is addressed to you, accept this new experience. Try to prevent yourself from perceiving only pain where there seems to be pain. Understand that pain is only painful at the level at which it is perceived; know that it is painful at that level, admit it is painful, then focus on the experience itself without judgment.

That's a lot of things to remember in the art of perfecting your listening skills! Let's move on to the art of perfecting your speech.

When you practiced RIN, you learned to adopt the attitude of trusting your right to speak, as well as your ability to speak. Never capitulate! You have to right to express yourself, but it does not imply that you must get your point of view across at any cost. It does not imply that you should battle until your vision of the information is assimilated by others; they have the right to their opinions too. It simply means that your spoken words have value, at least to yourself and your divinity. This being said, do not waste your precious speech when it is not being received. Trust yourself; before anything else, trust yourself.

As you learned in your studies of the KYO mind-set, take responsibility for what you say. Never lie by commission or omission; never be deceitful. To lie in whatever form is to condition your mind to believe that what you say is false and should not be manifested. This is a very poor habit to get into, if you hope to train your mind to manifest what you desire.

Therefore, always speak the truth, so that your mind is conditioned to trusting that what you say is true. Eventually, as you develop your powers of manifestation, you will say something and it will become true and manifest, if it is not already true. However, before you can manifest what you speak, you must establish this relationship of trust with your mind, by only speaking the truth. If you said something that implies you owe someone a service, act upon it and render the service, or affirm your incompetence and inform the concerned people that the service will not be rendered. Never allow a promise to be spoken that you do not fulfill according to your spoken word. Say "I Love You" only if it is true, but do not prevent yourself from saying it if such is genuinely the case. (Note: Do not be in a hurry to destroy your life, or your chances for happiness.)

As you learned with the TOH mind-set, be humble in choosing your words. Humility doesn't mean you have to suffer in silence. Most people confuse humility with shame or submission to someone who is exerting dominating control. Humility means that you are to remain in truth. If something should be said, then it must be said, and if something should not be said, then it must not be spoken. Some information serves a higher purpose when it is retained and other information is more useful when it is exchanged. To become Wise, one must develop a great discernment, especially in the choice of words, and whether to speak them or not.

As you learned with the SHA mind-set, always express yourself in a way that will lead to the accomplishment of your goal. Be powerful in your speech. Your words can become powerful by being whispered in the ears of a lover, or shouted at players on the game field (to encourage, not discourage), or elegantly recited on a stage, or pedagogically spoken from the dais in a lecture to a student. In every case, your words are to be clear and must always represent that which you wish to express. Practice using words as they are meant to be used; consider their meanings carefully and choose wisely. Do not hide behind sarcasm, lies, manipulations, or controversial arguments. Allow your words to express the power generated through your speech.

As you learned with the KAI mind-set, speak words of compassion and love. Do not express judgments and destructive criticism. Use your speech to express enlightenment and to bring enlightenment to yourself. Say beautiful things, and if this is hardly possible at certain times, at least say the truth. Do not degrade or lower the value of anyone, of anything, or any experience. If something does not fit you, there is always a good choice of words that will serve to rectify your experience. If there is no way to change what you are experiencing, it is useless to brag or complain about it unless it is to do self-therapy; self therapy must always make you a better person, in your heart. Express yourself when you are in pain, say the truth at the level you perceive it, but do not encourage the ego to play the victim game and do not amplify any situation with your words. Whenever possible, say happy words, funny jokes, accompanied with a smile, and define your life as a happy loving life. Life is meant to be enjoyed.

JIN Technique

Interlace all your fingers, with your fingertips inside, each of them touching the equivalent tip of the other hand's finger, if possible.

Chakra: Throat

Mantra jp: On aga na ya in ma ya sowaka

Mantra sk: Om agnaya yanmaya swaha

陣

Practice the JIN Kuji-In technique in its invocative manner, and listen to the words as you speak them. Listen to the physical vibration of the words. Notice that you are simultaneously speaking and listening to yourself. This is the obvious and simple part. After a few repetitions of paying attention to the actual words, begin to listen to more than one level at the same time. Listen to the physical level of vibration, and pay attention to the energy level of the words, the ethereal existence of the words you are speaking. Pay attention to both the physical and energetic level of the spoken mantra as you repeat it. Imagine that you are saying it at both levels. Using your visualization, imagine that there are many strata of vibrations layered one over the other, one inside the other, at the physical and energetic levels.

Speak simultaneously on both levels of vibration, and then listen to yourself at both these levels.

When you really feel you are speaking and listening at the energetic level, imagine a third layer of sound vibration in your mind without defining the specific level where it exists; just know that it is at a still higher level of vibration than the levels you were previously focused on. Once you feel you have imagined that level, continue to imagine more and more layers of sound, one over the other, one inside the other, without attempting to control the experience. Allow your experience to lead you. Vibrate the mantra at many levels of vibration, and listen to the many levels of vibration. At first, the most important part was to listen to the physical and energetic levels, even if that didn't really seem to work for you. Next, you must practice letting go of your control over the experience and focus on your multi-level connection with the sound vibrations.

Retsu

Retsu Way of Life

While you are gaining spiritual knowledge about yourself, you may begin to perceive that you are made out of different aspects of the same thing, (different levels of your existence as a human and spiritual entity). This awareness is triggered by the Jin technique and the activation of the throat chakra. Now that you are becoming aware of such realities, you might want to access them, to penetrate the different levels of consciousness, and the multiple space-time dimensions that comprise the Universe, each existing at their own frequency. Retsu opens the doorway which is found at the base of your skull. It sits inside the pointy bone at the back of the head. It is called the "Jade Gate". Thru this doorway, you may become aware of the spiritual realities and the forces behind all movements. It is the doorway between quantum physics and alchemy.

Let's say you are listening to a new song, one that you have never heard before, and you really like it. Your attitude is focused on that new song; perhaps you are caught up in your enthusiasm for the song, and you would not like to be disturbed by any other sounds around you. You are enjoying the rapture of discovering something new. This state of "availability" is blessed, since you are paying attention with joy to a new feeling, something you had not previously experienced. Once you listen to the song a few times, you might start to sing along with it, because you are really enjoying the song, yet, at the same time, you soon discover that your singing hinders this state of "availability". As soon as you started singing you became active, involved in the event, and thus controlling it. When you are active and controlling, you are not paying attention to the original song anymore. Obviously, when you are listening to a recorded song, it is something that is set in a specific and permanent pattern, it will not change, (the song will repeat over and over the same way). However, what would it be like for you if the song changed every time you heard it? What if it altered over time, producing new feelings in you, endlessly resulting in new discoveries? If such were the case, you would not sing over the song. You would keep on listening and paying attention.

I am pointing a specific state of mind that permits us to always be open to new discoveries, and, from that state, to discover what is before us: the changing, evolving, ever fresh world, experienced in joy. As children, we were almost permanently in this state of mind, rapt with enthusiasm at each discovery. If there were no discoveries at hand, we were filled with hope that one would soon come our way. This joy, this ability to be astonished at every little thing, this enthusiasm, is a necessary part of our spiritual attitude. Are you honestly astonished at the marvels of creation when you look at the corner of your dining room table? Are you speechless with astonishment before the miracle of your wonderful plastic fake-grass carpet? I am encouraging you to rediscover this ability to be impressed by all those things we take for granted. Once in a while, immerse yourself in something mundane. For example, gaze at the grain of something made of wood; be intentionally astonished at how it came to be so beautiful; give in and over-conceptualize about the flow of the One Life Force that created it.

Using this joyful attitude of discovery, pay attention to the different planes of existence, to the ebb and flow of energy around you, as well as to your own physical movements. Try to see those space-time dimensions you have been ignoring. It will probably take a while for you to start discerning them, but that is not the goal. The goal is simply to be able to be touched by the creation of God, thus accepting that there are realities that you are not yet aware of, thus releasing the control you constantly hold over your perceptive senses. This exercise will eventually make it possible for you to discern the many levels of consciousness and planes of existence. There is a time for listening, a time for speaking and a time for action. For now, simply listen without speaking, look without anticipating the next image, feel without moving around, and simply pay attention to the flow of creation, with joy.

Once the door (your Jade Gate) opens, the physical and spiritual space-time dimensions will reveal themselves to you. The laws of creation and manifestation will unveil themselves before your eyes. You will not have to work hard at it; you will simply be paying attention, available to anything new that comes into your field of awareness.

Retsu Technique

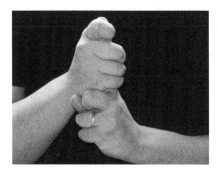 

Point your left index finger up. Wrap the fingers of your right hand around your left index finger. Place the tips of your right thumb and index finger in contact with the tip of your left index finger. The fingers of your left hand are gathered into a fist.

Chakra: Jade Gate, at the back of the head

Mantra jp: On hi ro ta ki sha no ga ji ba tai sowaka

Mantra sk: Om jyota-hi chandoga jiva tay swaha

列

While Retsu seems to be the simplest of all techniques, it is the one our human ego fights the most at the beginning. If you persist, your ego soon yields, collaborating with you on your path to assimilating new discoveries.

Perform the Retsu Kuji-In ritual technique. During the first step, do not visualize anything, simply focus on the designated areas.

For the first 3 to 9 mantras, pay attention to the Jade Gate, at the base of your skull. For the next 3 to 9 mantras, maintain your focus on the Jade Gate, simultaneously placing some of your attention on the middle of your back, between your shoulder blades, at the back of the heart charka. During the next 3 to 9 mantras, focus on all 3 areas, paying attention to the Jade Gate, the area at the back of your heart chakra, and your base chakra. Next, take a few deep silent breaths while maintaining your focus on all three (3) areas.

Finally, let go of all the visualizations, forget everything. Perform the ritual practice without any visualization, without counting …simply pay attention. Do not analyze, do not visualize, do not focus, do not take command, let yourself go. Pay attention to those dimensions that you don't normally perceive, even though you can't imagine what they would be like. Don't imagine them; don't invent them, simply pay attention. Do not force the previous focal points to close or open, to diminish or increase, simply allow everything to occur however it will. Do not get angry at your body's reaction, nor fight the images popping into your head, simply let everything go. This technique produces results every time, but you won't see those results for quite a while.

ZAI

ZAI Way of Life

ZAI is the path that leads beyond the illusion, takes you behind the veil, revealing the process of creation from which the experience of our human lives will inevitably unfold. It is from behind the veil that the creative forces of the Universe dance together, uniting to manifest the true desires that we have at the highest level of consciousness, (from the point of view of our Spirit). It is that place in our consciousness where we control what happens to us, whether we are aware of it or not.

Most of us spend our entire lives subject to Karmic Law, ignorantly living under the rule that yields shocking returns for our negative actions; it is under this rule that we continuously experience the consequences of our previous actions; and it is by our reactions to those actions that we keep the karmic wheel spinning. From this human point of view of our existence, we believe that what we desire, from our personal and individual role as human beings is what we really desire at all levels of our being. This error ignores the level of Spirit, which is ultimately the guiding force of our lives, and to which we are subject. In other words, simply put, it is our Spirit that "judges" us and that metes out our Karma so that we may evolve. Our human desires are subject to, and limited by the laws of nature, the instinct of survival, the rules of animal behavior. The Spirit is not limited in this way and can see the Grand Design. Yet, we are not to despise our own needs and wants. All that we seem to desire as a human *is still good for us*, since it serves our present human experience. We must accept ourselves as we are in our actual condition if we are to acquire a higher level of comprehension of our existence. By comprehending the position of the self to the Spirit, and accepting the role of each, it is possible to evolve. That said, for students on a spiritual path, it is important to pay more attention to our spiritual existence.

What we seek on the path of ZAI is to become aware of the act of creation that we constantly use (on the Spiritual level) in total free will. With absolute free will, we can manifest all that we truly wish for, simply by desiring it at the level of Spirit. With free will, we are free, and our will becomes reality. The creative elements of the Universe naturally agglomerate around the desires of an awakened Spirit; this causes the desires to become denser, and more material until they become available to the human experience (manifest as reality).

Unfortunately, our free will is usually buried under the weight of our egotistical need to control everything. We must accept this fact if we are to elevate ourselves beyond it; we must not use this as a reason to remain limited by our human behaviors. We must be courageous, face the unknown and become aware of our existence as Spirit. As human animals, we are subject to the laws of the Universe. As Divine Spirits, even though we are enmeshed in daily human experience, we have a "human share" of Divine power that is available to us at anytime. It takes some practice, wisdom, determination and faith to apply the techniques that will eventually lead to our power to create.

All the Kuji-In techniques that we have learned up to now have served this ultimate goal: to give us back our Divine power, including: our faith, our self-love, and the tools we need to interact with the Universe and to create our reality in conformity with our desire. By using these Kuji-In techniques, we have learned to be in charge, to accept the truth as it is, yet to change it anyway. We have practiced observing our experience and learned to work at making it better. Even though we remain the cause of our own deception (each time we blame others for what happens to us) by taking back our responsibility for everything that we experience, we are freeing our minds from the hold of the ego that believes IT has control over our destiny. This awakening releases our Divine free will, and permits our initial power of manifestation to occur naturally with harmony between Spirit and Consciousness.

Even though all spiritual seekers are anxious to become the ultimate creators of their own lives, it is not wise to rush into formulating desires for our Spirit to fulfill, because, in these first attempts, it would only be our ego trying to impose its vision on our Spirit (once again). Our Spirit, out of respect for our free will, would gladly accept those newly formulated ego-contrived-goals, letting us fall (once again) into the need to suffer from the negative fallout of our limited experience and understanding. Our human ego is actually our best friend (and a good teacher) on the spiritual path, but we must not allow our human identity to proclaim itself as Divine. God will be God in ITS own experience of ITSELF, and our Spirit already has a plethora of wonderful desires for us, ready to manifest in our lives at any time, with abundance and joy, directly from the realm where we are all one with God.

This can only happen when we accept that, as humans, we are not in control. We will have control over our lives only by elevating our definition of ourselves. The ZAI way of life consists of working with our mind, heart and body in order to define ourselves as a Spirit that is having a human experience, rather than a human being sometimes having a spiritual experience. Do not make the mistake of discarding your human identity, the results would be disastrous. Instead, remember that your human identity is a necessary part of your experience of yourself as a Spirit, and that it is from the point of view of the Spirit that everything has occurred right from your birth. Only a human is arrogant enough to try to eradicate himself from God's design, but God knows us, God created us, and man cannot eradicate himself; it is best to accept the plan, understand the plan, and to come into harmony what it is. God sees through our eyes. Even though we are bemoaning our fate, God does not see separation or conflict while watching this journey though our eyes. It is merely the ego that gets upset when it realizes that the idea that it was ever in charge of anything is mere illusion. Redefine yourself as a Divine being experiencing human life, and cherish your human experience; each life experience has great value. The human identity you have forged over time is the treasure that you bring to your Divine Self as you awaken to your spiritual existence. It is who you truly are. Whatever you do, whatever you know or think you know, you are still YOU and you have never stopped, nor will you ever stop being yourself. It is only *your point of view* that changes. The level at which you perceive yourself evolves. At the same time, as Spirit, you are in charge of everything, and you are a servant of your human self. Now, all you have to do is to decide which point of view you wish to exist from.

Zai Technique

Touch the tips of your thumbs
and index fingers to form a
triangle, while your other
fingers are spread out.

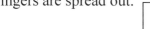

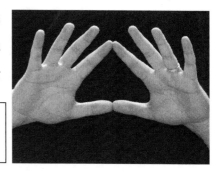

Chakra: Third Eye

Mantra jp: On Chi ri Chi i ba ro ta ya sowaka

Mantra sk: Om srija iva rtaya swaha

The Universe is composed of many levels of vibration resulting from a single holy experience. We have practiced gently closing one realm of reality, so that we could pay attention to the many other realms, physical to spiritual, that are part of our existence. Now, it is time to look at the Creator's work of art and to observe the Grand Plan. Pay attention to the dance of the elements used to create the Universe. ZAI is a prayer for a revelation of truth. ZAI asks that your Spirit show you what you are in totality, as well as what the Universe is and how it operates.

The original elements, of which everything is made, assemble themselves and condense according to the laws governing the spiritual act of manifestation. The traditional (and widespread) belief is that a side effect of this Kuji-In technique might eventually be the ability to influence some of nature's manifestations, such as the movement of rain and wind. However, those details fall into the global scope of becoming the "Creator" again. Don't waste time trying to make it rain unless it is necessary for your training. A true master never, or rarely cares about such details. The ZAI technique is meant to get us back in touch with our ability to create. It is not the operation of manifestation *in itself* with which we are concerned here. The actual method of manifestation will naturally follow the initial reconciliation of our human identity with its Spiritual authority. For now, we can't build if we don't have the tools.

You never know how a revelation will occur. We do not have human control over such spiritual events. Perform the ZAI Kuji-In while you focus on your third eye, and simply get in touch with the free elements of creation at the spiritual level, as well as their denser counterparts on the human and physical levels. After a shorter or more extended period of time, which depends on how elevated a point of view you attained during your practice, a revelation may occur to you and you will know a bit more about yourself and the Universe.

Where Human and Spirit Touch

Compassion is our human ability to see the lesson in a painful human experience and, while we understand the painful experience, having compassion means that we wish to support the one afflicted by it and to offer them comfort. Sometimes we are the human who is in need of comfort and compassion; therefore, in a painful situation, we may justifiably offer compassion to our own human heart. This process is one way we have found of bringing some comfort to ourselves, even though we still wish to resolve the pain by developing a correct understanding of the situation and undertaking a series of rectifying actions.

The highest and purest emotion a human being can feel is compassion, which comes from your most holy experience of life; when you attain the ultimate devotion to the highest good for yourself, from a state of pure Love, you have achieved the emotion of compassion.

The most horrible, dense, degraded, separated, painful, destructive and darkest emotion a Spirit can feel is... compassion.

Compassion is the lowest point of the Spirit and the highest point of the human, and it is at that juncture where they meet and become one. Compassion is therefore the doorway to power, the ultimate link between the Divine and human world. It is there, at the place where we experience compassion that the exchange between Spirit and human is the most powerful. When this connection is made, the powerful flow from above and below is unblocked, and is allowed to flow freely in both directions.

From the human point of view, compassion is the point of view where pain cannot possibly exist, where all painful and pleasurable sensations are merely felt as information about our human experiences. It is the place where we look at our entire human experience and see only the lessons of love. It is from that place that a human being can understand the point of view of Spirit.

For Spirit, compassion is the point of view where pain might possibly exist, where all the information which is felt as a result of our human experience could become tainted with the polarity of good and evil, pleasure and pain. It is from that place that Spirit can grasp the totality of human experience, and embrace it with love and understanding.

Learn what it is to have compassion. Learn how to act with compassion. Practice switching your point of view from an afflicted human to a comprehensive Spirit, and, even then, continue to step into action to resolve unwanted human experiences. Do not deny your own pain under the false pretext that you are above it. Simply switch point of views, and the pain will transform itself over time.

ZEN

ZEN Way of Life

Step 1

Zen's way of life is a challenging proposition and will require quite a long time before you are able to attain proficiency with the technique. Nevertheless, even your initial attempts to practice this technique will transform your life. Fixity meditation is adequate, by itself, to assist you in becoming aware of the spiritual aspects of your life, so that you can feel the energies in your body when you return from your meditative state.

Practice meditation often. You should meditate a few minutes after each Kuji-In practice. In fact, you should consider adding meditation to your daily routine, even if you are only able to do it for a few minutes every day. The more you meditate, the faster your growth will occur hereafter. Meditate 10 minutes, 20 minutes, even 30 minutes at a sitting. Practice keeping your body in a meditative state for longer and longer periods of time. When meditating, hold still as long as you can without paying attention to the little physical disturbances: itching, cramps, tingling.

The more you meditate, the more powerful your ability to manifest what you think and desire will become. Thus, when you return to an awake and aware state, focus only on the things you wish for, or on the things that make you happy. Discarding this rule can turn your life into a living hell, while respecting this rule can turn it into heaven.

Fixity meditation

Fixity Meditation consists of gazing at something without really look at it. Fixity can be performed by focusing on a point in front of you, or on the floor a little ways away. You may recite a mantra mentally to keep your mind focused and to profit from the effects of the mantra. You may drop off using the mantra anywhere in the meditation, as soon as you are sure that you can maintain a state of mental inactivity and are able to keep your gaze fixed on whatever you have chosen. I recommend a blank wall.

A simple fixity meditation:
- Begin with the breathing technique of your choice for 2 minutes.
- Use a mental mantra of your choice for 2 to 5 minutes.

- Practice fixity, eyes opened, using no mantra, from 5 to 45 minutes. No mind, no word, no image.

After you have put in some time and practice, you will realize that your consciousness has been in an altered state, because of the changes in consciousness you feel when you come out of the meditative state. The ultimate goal of meditation is to transcend consciousness and yet, to remain conscious at the same time. However, you must train your body and mind to transcend consciousness one step at a time.

The first sign of a successful meditation is the slumber that happens naturally when you relax so much that you let your body go to sleep while spiritual energies enter your energy channels. Your body will fall asleep and you will feel sleepy when you return to consciousness. This means that you slept and did not transcend. Still, it is a good thing since it is a normal part of the practice. At this point your body and energy channels are getting used to receiving spiritual energies. Do what you can to remain awake while you meditate, but slumber is inevitable at first.

After you have practiced this exercise for a while you will no longer succumb to sleep. You may lose consciousness for a moment or two, but you will always return to your bodily awareness and then immediately notice that your body maintained its posture all by itself. You will also notice that you do not feel sleepy. This is because you did not fall asleep, so you are not waking up. You will feel that your consciousness is altered in some way; you will feel light, energetic and ready to go on with your daily affairs.

You will quickly become comfortable being in an altered state of consciousness and you will also become increasingly aware of the spiritual sensations in your physical body. Eventually, you might notice that the altered consciousness and spiritual sensations occur, but you did not lose consciousness at all during the entire meditation. This means you transcended consciously and that you have achieved a great transformation in your body. You will probably alternate between conscious and unconscious transcendence from one meditation to the next, depending on your level of fatigue and state of mind. Do not worry about it, only illumed masters transcend consciously at will.

Step 2

The second step of ZEN's way, is to maintain yourself in this spiritual attitude as long as possible, while, at the same time, remaining totally conscious of your physical reality. Attempt to maintain a spiritual attitude in all of your actions, at every moment.

When you complete a meditation or spiritual technique, try to remain in the altered state of consciousness resulting from your meditation, but ground yourself in your physical body as much as possible. You will want to adopt an attitude which permits your Spirit to inhabit your body at all times. This requires that you are able to achieve a meditative state at the same time that you are focusing on the physical actions you must perform. Move slowly at first, repeat your mantra mentally if needed.

You may feel a bit dizzy from time to time. You may also have the odd experience of feeling that you don't belong in this reality. You might have short moments of intense distraction or even lose consciousness of the physical plane of reality for a few seconds. You will need to develop an attitude where it is wonderful to have a physical body and live in this world, as this is something that is very difficult to do while transcending. This is why you must be careful and work on this technique at appropriate times, in appropriate places.

Do not try to work on a meditative or spiritual technique while you are driving a car, or when a transcendent state could cause injury to yourself or someone else. Do not practice this technique while you are working at a construction site. Never do it at work, where your efficiency might be hindered by a momentary transcendence. Apply this technique only whenever you can permit yourself to lose focus for a few seconds. The ultimate goal is to practice remaining spiritually transcendent at all times, but it is best to begin with the safest environment and the most relaxed practice period. Never put yourself in situations where you could injure yourself or others. Do not do this technique when you are with too many people, or when you could be judged by others if you transcend in public. Keep your practices for yourself and apply this technique when it is easy to apply, where there will be no negative consequence as a result of the possible reactions of your body and mind to the technique.

ZEN technique

Rest your left knuckles on the fingers of your right hand, with your right palm open. Touch the tips of your two thumbs gently.

前

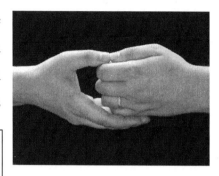

Chakra: Crown

Mantra jp: On a ra ba sha no-o sowaka

Mantra sk: Om ah ra pa cha na dhi

It is believed that your chakra system and the central energy channel of your body are very much like a conduit that allows energy to flow in and out of your energy system. It is easy to imagine a series of tubes with energy flowing into us and out of us. We may leap to the conclusion that, if something can flow through this conduit, it must be empty, but this erroneous deduction is the result of the stilted observations available to us as a result of the restricted data from our limited senses and our limited experience.

Your chakra system and what we call its central channel are not channels at all. The nature of your chakra system is greatly superior to a series of wires and tubes: in fact your chakra system is made out of "consciousness". The chakra system is not a physical body, nor it is a hose through which energy runs; it is a conscious spirit which resides at the core of your body.

Each chakra is a state of consciousness that is designed to sample the different flavors and experiences of life. Each chakra is a sensory instrument of the soul which is extended into our physical body so that our Spirit can experience life at every level. Energy resonates thru the chakras, rather than flowing through them.

For example, in a radio speaker, electricity is used to vibrate a magnet, which in turn makes the air vibrate, generating sound. There are no actual electrons or pieces of the magnet flying around for us to hear; what we hear are intangible vibrations. With regard to eyesight, we perceive photoelectric radiations emitted from the sun or a light bulb, but there are no chunks of light bulbs or hydrogen particles in fusion flying around that our eyeballs grab onto somehow. We SEE because our eyes respond to vibrations, the vibration of photons.

It is correct to say that energy, in the form of Qi, Jing and Shen, flows thru our energy system, into our energy meridians. It is also correct to say that energy flows through our chakras. But our chakras are not tubes; they are not hollow; they are not empty; yet they are not filled either; they are levels of "consciousness".

The Zen technique is simple. Perform the Kuji-In practice while paying attention to the consciousness inside you, rather than the energy in your body.

Begin this technique by focusing only on your breathing. Sustain enough mental awareness of the ritual technique that you are able to keep up with the (mudra, mantra, mandala), but focus mainly on your breathing for a few minutes.

Pay attention to your entire physical body for another few minutes, and then focus on your feelings and emotions for a few minutes. If you have no sensation of feelings or emotions (good, you are at peace) then concentrate your attention on the process of feeling your mental body. Continue putting your attention on your mind and mental activity. Do not encourage any particular thoughts; simply focus on your mental body, the concept of thinking, the actual processes themselves.

Finally, pay attention to your consciousness, your spirit, your soul or whatever notion of your spiritual existence you can grasp. Slowly drop each aspect of the Kuji-In technique, one after the other. Drop the mudra and place your hands on your lap or in meditation position, as you continue the meditation. Slowly repeat the prayer mantra mentally, and gaze. Be aware of yourself as Spirit. Become your consciousness and let yourself transcend in meditation.

Proceeding through the levels of breathing, bodily awareness, feeling, mental awareness and spiritual awareness, you have climbed the ladder of awareness up through the different states of consciousness of your body and self, to that place where you can finally praise the Divine Spirit that you are.

The 9-Day Kuji-in Meditative Process

Each day for nine straight days, at approximately the same time each day, perform the following ritual using only one Kuji-in step per day:

- Active Qi-Gong technique of your choice, 2 minutes.
- Air and Energy Breathing technique, 2 minutes.
- Daily Kuji-In technique, invocative, 2 minutes.
- Daily Kuji-In technique, meditative, 15-20 minutes.
- Come back to your conscious awareness and contemplate silently, 2 minutes.

The first day, you will only use the RIN technique. The second day, perform RIN only 3 times and then quickly concentrate on the KYO technique. The third day, perform RIN 3 times, then KYO 3 times, then focus on the TOH technique, and so on until, on the ninth day, you will perform each technique 3 times and then focus on the ZEN technique. Perform each technique to the best of your ability.

The experienced student may either complete the ritual twice daily, (morning and evening), or you may double the length of time for each step. This 9-day process will initiate a new level of practice and understanding of the entire Kuji-In System. As you practice every nuance of the listening and speaking exercises, you will see your life transform right before your eyes. You will become happier and more fulfilled. By remaining available to every type of knowledge at every level, you will gain much more knowledge than what is transmitted to you by your five senses. You will learn simply by listening, by watching, by contemplating, by allowing the truth to reveal itself to you. When you achieve this level of accomplishment, then, when you speak, only beautiful experiences will occur as a result of what you have said.

The 63-Hour Kuji-in Self-Initiation Process

The ultimate Kuji-In experience is usually passed on to a student in the context of an Initiation which is performed under the guidance of a Master. However, there are many students who do not have direct access to a Master in a Temple, yet who may still desire to have the experience of Initiation. In order to be able to have a genuine Initiation experience, the student must learn how to raise their energy sufficiently to enable them to receive the transformative experience that is a fundamental part of an authentic Kuji-In Initiation: they must experience the phenomena of revelation that cannot be expressed with words.

This Initiation experience should not be attempted by any student until the student is thoroughly conversant with the entire Kuji-In system. Attempts to rush such a process will be fruitless. However, for those who have put an earnest effort into learning the steps, this 63 hour process will produce an astonishing amount of energy. Although the Initiation process will most certainly produce the desired transformative effects, this intensive initiatic gauntlet may also manifest a multitude of unusual physical reactions in the student. It should therefore be used only when you honestly feel ready for such an experience.

You should terminate the process the moment you feel: too much pain; a loss of eyesight or hearing (even for a moment); troubling visions, or if you have any intensely troubling or unbearably painful experience.

When you begin this process, be absolutely certain that you are in a safe place where you will not be disturbed for the duration of the Initiation. Set up the area where you will be performing the Initiation so that you will not be injured if you fall to the floor. Do not be surprised if you experience a few mild electric shocks and do not give up at the first sign of discomfort. Please understand that everyone has a different experience with the Kuji-In Initiation. In fact, every student has a unique experience with the entire Kuji-In transformative process because of the diversity of the traditions and applications which comprise it.

The process is simplicity itself: Practice RIN for 7 hours. This may be accomplished by performing the RIN Kuji one hour each day for seven days, or 3.5 hours for two (2) consecutive days, or continuously for seven (7) hours (all in one day). Once you have completed the RIN Kuji series, you will do the same for KYO, TOH, SHA... until you have completed 63 hours of Kuji-In training in no more than 63 days.

In order for this process to be successful, you should not skip even one day of practice during the Self-Initiation. However, if you begin to experience too many uncomfortable physical symptoms, slow the process down to one hour per day. If you find that even that is too hard on you, you are not yet ready for the Initiation and you should return to building up your energy system by using the normal practice. Once you feel that you are better prepared, you may re-start the process a few weeks later.

For each practice period you will perform:

- The Active Qi-Gong technique of your choice, 2 minutes.
- Air and Energy Breathing technique, 2 minutes.
- Kuji-In invocative technique (Length determined by your plan).
- Silent contemplation after your practice for the day.

Conclusion: self-transformation

It has been a while now, that we behave the way we do. It has been a long time since the beginning of humanity. From the animal origins of our body, up to the pretentious assertion that we are sentient and knowledgeable of many great secrets, the genetic foundation of our human life still has a lot to do with the way we act, and react.

It will take some effort, and comfort, to become aware of all that we are, and consciously take back the mastery of our own experience of life. But we are not alone, and we are not left without help. We firmly hold the tools that will serve us in our quest. With a balance of practical application and self contemplation, we will succeed in remembering who we are, by acknowledging the truth as it is revealed to us from within.

The goal of our path is to transform ourselves, starting down from our deepest foundations, into the root of our existence, to free ourselves from our apparent bodily shell and to redefine ourselves as the glorious living experience of the Spirit. As we advance on the path, the transformation looks more like a remembering of what we left behind when we came to be human.

We work ceaselessly to sublimate the inner workings of our mind and our body; to accept our human animal being as the beauty of creation, although we thrive to remember our wondrous spiritual origin.

I pray that you will have to courage to apply the techniques and the wisdom long enough for it to unveil the treasures it carries. I pray that you will find yourself, that you will remember who you are, and that you will look unto yourself as the wonderful being you created at the moment of your own origin.

Be blessed, seeker of the truth,

Maha Vajra

Made in the USA
Columbia, SC
15 March 2018